★ THE ★
UNITED
STATES
PRESIDENTS

JOHN QUINCY
ADAMS

Heidi M.D. Elston

Checkerboard
Library

An Imprint of Abdo Publishing
abdobooks.com

★ ★ ★

ABDOBOOKS.COM

Published by Abdo Publishing, a division of ABDO, PO Box 398166, Minneapolis, Minnesota 55439. Copyright © 2021 by Abdo Consulting Group, Inc. International copyrights reserved in all countries. No part of this book may be reproduced in any form without written permission from the publisher. Checkerboard Library™ is a trademark and logo of Abdo Publishing.

Printed in the United States of America, North Mankato, Minnesota
052020
092020

THIS BOOK CONTAINS
RECYCLED MATERIALS

Design: Emily O'Malley, Kelly Doudna, Mighty Media, Inc.
Production: Mighty Media, Inc.
Editor: Liz Salzmann

Cover Photograph: Getty Images
Interior Photographs: Albert de Bruijn/iStockphoto, p. 37; AP Images, p. 36; Classic Image/Alamy, p. 31; Getty Images, pp. 21, 28, 32; Hulton Archive/Getty Images, p. 27; Library of Congress, pp. 6 (Louisa Adams), 14, 16, 17, 29, 33, 40; National Archives, pp. 7 (Treaty of Ghent), 18 (Treaty of Ghent), 20; National Park Service, pp. 6 (birthplace), 11 (birthplace), 15; North Wind Picture Archives, pp. 6, 7, 11, 18, 19, 25; North Wind Picture Archives/Alamy, p. 23; OCLC Preservation Service Center/Massachusetts Historical Society, p. 30; Pete Souza/Flickr, p. 44; The Print Collector/Alamy, p. 12; Shutterstock Images, pp. 13, 38, 39; Wikimedia Commons, pp. 5, 7 (John Q. Adams portrait), 40 (George Washington), 42

Library of Congress Control Number: 2019956437

Publisher's Cataloging-in-Publication Data
Names: Elston, Heidi M.D., author.
Title: John Quincy Adams / by Heidi M.D. Elston
Description: Minneapolis, Minnesota : Abdo Publishing, 2021 | Series: The United States presidents |
    Includes online resources and index.
Identifiers: ISBN 9781532193385 (lib. bdg.) | ISBN 9781098212025 (ebook)
Subjects: LCSH: Adams, John Quincy, 1767-1848--Juvenile literature. | Presidents--Biography--
    Juvenile literature. | Presidents--United States--History--Juvenile literature. | Legislators--
    United States—Biography--Juvenile literature. | Politics and government--Biography--Juvenile
    literature.
Classification: DDC 973.55092--dc23

★ CONTENTS ★

John Quincy Adams

John Quincy Adams was the sixth president of the United States. His father, John Adams, was the second US president. This was the first time a son of a former US president had become president.

As a young man, Adams was a lawyer and a writer. These experiences helped him start his political career as a successful **diplomat**. Later, Adams was elected to the US Senate. He also worked as **secretary of state**.

Adams served one term as president. President Adams fought for what he believed was right. Along the way, he made many political enemies. They kept Adams from making improvements to the country he felt were necessary.

Following his time as president, Adams served 17 years in the US House of Representatives. There, he fought the spread of slavery in the United States.

Throughout his adult life, Adams served his country at home and abroad. His work helped change the nation for the better. Today, Adams is remembered as one of America's greatest diplomats.

John Quincy Adams

★ TIMELINE ★

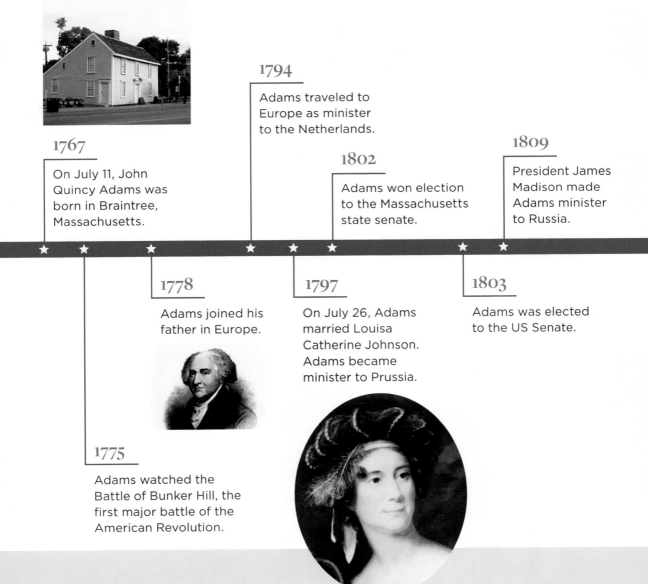

1794
Adams traveled to Europe as minister to the Netherlands.

1767
On July 11, John Quincy Adams was born in Braintree, Massachusetts.

1802
Adams won election to the Massachusetts state senate.

1809
President James Madison made Adams minister to Russia.

1778
Adams joined his father in Europe.

1797
On July 26, Adams married Louisa Catherine Johnson. Adams became minister to Prussia.

1803
Adams was elected to the US Senate.

1775
Adams watched the Battle of Bunker Hill, the first major battle of the American Revolution.

Treaty of
Peace and Amity
between
His Britannic Majesty
and
The United States of America

1814

Adams worked to get the Treaty of Ghent signed. This ended the War of 1812.

1815

Adams began serving as minister to Great Britain.

1817

President James Monroe appointed Adams secretary of state.

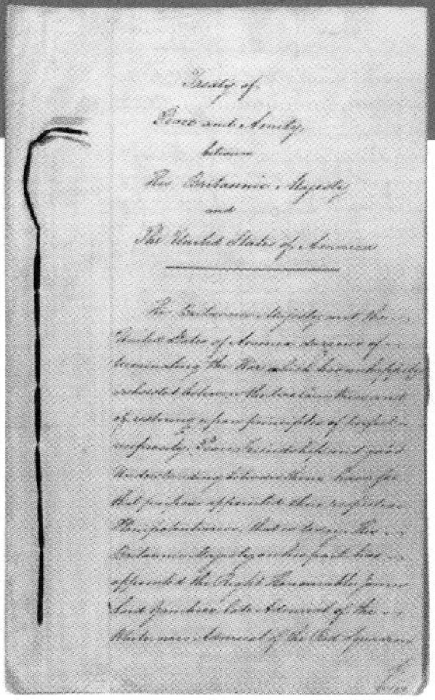

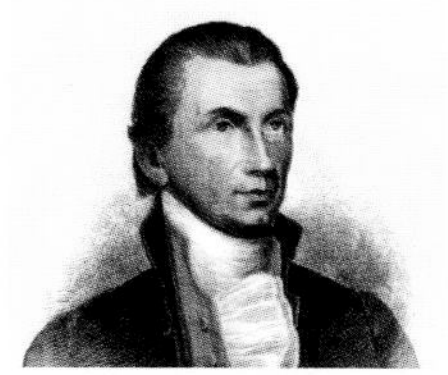

1823

Adams helped write the Monroe Doctrine.

1825

On March 4, Adams became the sixth US president.

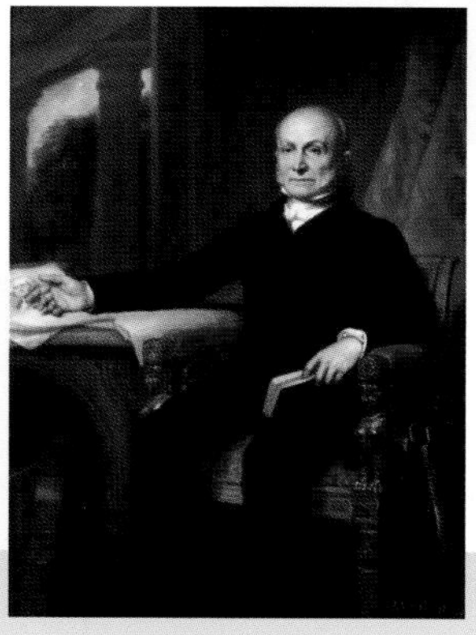

1828

Adams placed a tariff on imported industrial goods.

1830

Adams was elected to the US House of Representatives.

1841

Adams defended the *Amistad* captives.

1848

On February 23, John Quincy Adams died.

" From the experience
of the past we derive

**instructive lessons
for the future.**"

DID YOU KNOW?

★ John Quincy Adams was the first president sworn in while wearing long pants. The first five presidents wore knickers, which are short, loose-fitting pants gathered at the knee.

★ On warm mornings, President Adams swam in the Potomac River. One day, reporter Anne Royall surprised him there. She sat on his clothes and refused to move until he gave her an interview. Before this, no female had interviewed a president.

★ Adams lived long enough to see the camera invented. Toward the end of his life, he had his picture taken. He is the first president of whom a photograph exists.

★ Louisa Adams is one of two first ladies born outside of the United States. The other is Melania Trump.

Witnessing History

John Quincy Adams was born on July 11, 1767, in Braintree, Massachusetts. The town was later renamed Quincy. John Quincy was the oldest son of John and Abigail Adams. He had an older sister and two younger brothers.

Young John Quincy saw US history being made. He and his mother watched the Battle of Bunker Hill near the family farm in 1775. It was the first major battle of the **American Revolution**.

During the war, John Quincy's parents provided most of his education. John told young John Quincy about events that had led to the start of the American Revolution. This included the Boston **Massacre** in 1770. During a **riot** in Boston, Massachusetts, British soldiers shot and killed five colonists. John had defended the soldiers in court.

FAST FACTS

BORN: July 11, 1767

WIFE: Louisa Catherine Johnson (1775–1852)

CHILDREN: 4

POLITICAL PARTY: Democratic-Republican

AGE AT INAUGURATION: 57

YEARS SERVED: 1825–1829

VICE PRESIDENT: John C. Calhoun

DIED: February 23, 1848, age 80

The oldest presidential birthplaces in the United States are in Quincy, Massachusetts. They are the John Quincy Adams birthplace (*left*) and the John Adams birthplace (*right*).

Abigail Adams ——— ——— John Adams

John also told John Quincy about the Boston Tea Party. Colonists protested a tea tax in 1773. They dumped 342 chests of British tea into Boston Harbor.

In 1778, John went to Europe as a **diplomat**. John Quincy joined him. He lived throughout Europe for most of his teenage years.

From 1778 to 1779, John Quincy studied at a private school in Paris, France. There, he became **fluent** in French. John Quincy spent the next year at the University of Leiden in the Netherlands. During his brief stay, he became fluent in Dutch.

When he was 14, John Quincy went to Russia with Francis Dana. Dana was US minister to Russia. John Quincy worked as his assistant. One year later, John Quincy joined his father in Paris. He helped John with the treaty that ended the **American Revolution**. This is called the Treaty of Paris.

In 1785, John Quincy returned to America. He had been well

Young John Quincy

Harvard University is the oldest
university in the United States.

taught in history, mathematics, and classical languages
such as Latin and Greek. John Quincy entered Harvard
College in Cambridge, Massachusetts. He graduated in just
two years.

After college, John Quincy decided to study law. In
1790, he became a lawyer. John Quincy then struggled to
set up a law practice. Meanwhile, he began writing political
newspaper articles. His articles caught President George
Washington's attention.

Diplomat

President Washington liked John Quincy's writings and made him minister to the Netherlands. In May 1794, Adams sailed to Europe to begin his **diplomatic** career. As minister, he reported to President Washington on events in the Netherlands and other European countries. Washington would later use some of Adams's phrases in his farewell address in 1796.

As part of his duties, Adams also traveled to London, England, to conduct government business with the British Foreign Office. On one of his London trips, Adams met Louisa

Louisa Adams

Catherine Johnson. She was charming, warm, and well educated. Adams and Louisa were married on July 26, 1797.

Earlier that year, Adams's father had become the second US President. He made Adams minister to Prussia. So, Adams and Louisa moved to Prussia's capital, Berlin. There, Adams helped write a treaty with Prussia. He also traveled with his wife through Europe.

Mr. and Mrs. Adams's first child, George Washington Adams,

George Washington Adams

was born in Berlin in 1801. He was named after President Washington. Later that year, the Adams family returned to Boston. There, Adams briefly worked as a lawyer.

Senator Adams

Soon, **Adams decided to work in politics.** In 1802, he was elected to the Massachusetts state senate. The next year, Adams won election to the US Senate.

In 1807, President Thomas Jefferson called for a shipping **embargo**. Senator Adams supported the president. This action made him unpopular in New England. People there depended on shipping to make money. The next year, Adams quit the Senate.

Meanwhile, Mr. and Mrs. Adams had two more sons. John was born in 1803, and Charles Francis followed in 1807. A daughter named Louisa Catherine was born in 1811. Sadly, she died the next year.

In 1809, President James Madison made Adams minister to Russia. There, Adams saw French emperor Napoléon Bonaparte invade the country. As minister, Adams stayed in Europe to work for peace.

President Thomas Jefferson

Like his father, Charles Francis also became a politician. He was a state senator. He ran for vice-president in 1848 but lost the election.

The Sixth President

A record of the 1824 Electoral College votes

Adams did well as **secretary of state.** Many historians consider Adams the finest secretary of state in American history.

In 1824, Adams decided to run for president as a **Democratic-Republican**. Adams was one of five candidates. His opponents were **Secretary of the Treasury** William H. Crawford and **Speaker of the House** Henry Clay. Adams was also up against General Andrew Jackson and **Secretary of War** John C. Calhoun. Calhoun eventually withdrew from the contest and ran for vice president.

Like his father, Charles Francis also became a politician. He was a state senator. He ran for vice-president in 1848 but lost the election.

Secretary Adams

America and Great Britain fought each other in the **War of 1812**. In August 1814, Adams and a group of Americans went to Ghent, Belgium. They wanted to make peace with the British. Four months later, the Treaty of Ghent was signed.

Beginning in 1815, Adams served as minister to Great Britain. He and his family lived in a country house near London.

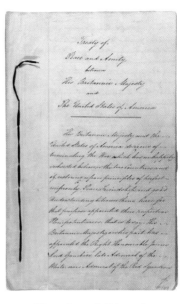

— Treaty of Ghent —

Adams returned to the United States in 1817. President James Monroe made him **secretary of state**.

At that time, Spain owned the Florida Territory. Adams made a deal with Spanish leaders. Spain agreed to give Florida to the United States. This was a great victory for the United States and for Adams.

— President James Monroe —

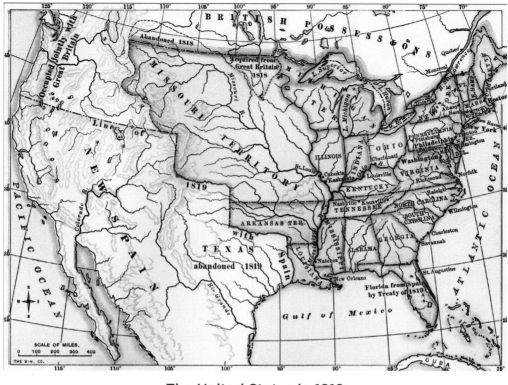

The United States in 1819

Secretary Adams's **diplomatic** success continued. In 1823, he helped write the Monroe Doctrine. It said that the United States supported North and South American colonies against European interference. Also, the United States would not allow Europeans to create new colonies in the Americas.

The Sixth President

A record of the 1824
Electoral College votes

Adams did well as **secretary of state**. Many historians consider Adams the finest secretary of state in American history.

In 1824, Adams decided to run for president as a **Democratic-Republican**. Adams was one of five candidates. His opponents were **Secretary of the Treasury** William H. Crawford and **Speaker of the House** Henry Clay. Adams was also up against General Andrew Jackson and **Secretary of War** John C. Calhoun. Calhoun eventually withdrew from the contest and ran for vice president.

Going into the election, Adams had the
support of the New England states.

Jackson received 99 electoral votes. Adams won 84 votes, Crawford received 41, and Clay won 37. To win, a candidate needed more than half the total votes. None of the men had enough.

According to the US **Constitution**, the House of Representatives now had to choose the president. The House chose from the top three candidates. That meant Clay was out of the race.

Clay decided to back Adams. With Clay's support, Adams was elected the sixth US president in February 1825. Calhoun won the vice presidency. On March 4, Adams was sworn into office.

President Adams wanted the best advisers for his **cabinet**. He refused to choose people based on the political party they belonged to.

Adams chose Clay as his **secretary of state**. Jackson's supporters in Congress protested. They claimed that Clay had helped Adams get elected so they could both get into office. Now, President Adams had political enemies in Congress.

Vice President Calhoun

PRESIDENT ADAMS'S CABINET

ONE TERM
March 4, 1825–March 4, 1829

- ★ **STATE:** Henry Clay
- ★ **TREASURY:** Richard Rush
- ★ **WAR:** James Barbour
  Peter B. Porter (from June 21, 1828)
- ★ **NAVY:** Samuel Lewis Southard
- ★ **ATTORNEY GENERAL:** William Wirt

Secretary of State Henry Clay

Running the Country

President Adams wanted to advance America. In his **inaugural** address, he laid out a plan for many improvements. He wanted to build new roads and canals. He proposed establishing a national university and **observatory**. And, he wanted new laws to protect Native Americans.

But President Adams still had many political enemies. Congress rejected most of his ideas. However, he did succeed in extending the Cumberland Road into Ohio. This road eventually stretched from Cumberland, Maryland, to Vandalia, Illinois. It opened up the West to settlement.

In 1828, President Adams signed a bill placing a **tariff** on imported industrial goods. Adams believed the tax would protect New England factories from foreign competition. Northerners supported the tariff, but Southerners opposed it. The tariff would become a key issue in the 1828 election.

SUPREME COURT APPOINTMENT

ROBERT TRIMBLE: 1826

Throughout his presidency, Adams maintained a daily exercise routine. In the mornings, he swam in the Potomac River. He took long walks in the evenings. Adams also wrote daily in his diary and spent much time reading the Bible.

Although President Adams kept busy, he was sad about his battles with Congress. Adams held little hope for reelection in 1828.

Throughout his presidency, Adams's quarrels with Jackson continued.

The Election of 1828

In 1828, President Adams was part of one of the ugliest elections in US history. He ran as a **National Republican**. Adams's **running mate** was **Secretary of the Treasury** Richard Rush.

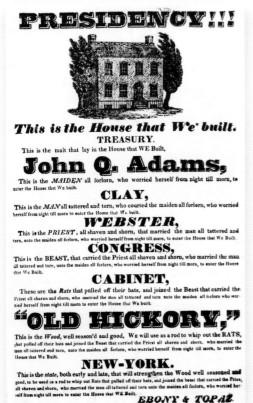

An election poster for Jackson

Andrew Jackson ran as a **Democrat**. Vice President Calhoun was Jackson's running mate.

The campaign was hateful. Both sides launched political and personal attacks against each other. The attacks harmed Adams's campaign. Jackson successfully won over most of the country. Adams had too many political enemies to win the election. Jackson received 178 electoral votes, and Adams won 83.

Adams took his defeat hard. He refused to attend Jackson's **inauguration**. In 1829, Adams returned to Quincy, Massachusetts.

Andrew Jackson

Old Man Eloquent

Following his time as president, Adams planned to retire. But in 1830, he was elected to the US House of Representatives. He served in the House for the rest of his life.

Adams had not been a popular president. But he was well liked and respected as a representative. Many congressmen admired the feeling he showed in his speeches. They called Adams "Old Man Eloquent."

In Congress, Adams fought slavery. Congressmen from the South passed a series of gag rules. These rules banned any talk of slavery in the House. The gag rules kept laws against slavery from being passed. Adams fought the gag rules for eight years. Congress finally ended them in 1844.

Adams wrote in his diary about his election to the US House of Representatives.

Even when he faced bitter opposition, Adams fought for what he believed was right.

In 1841, Representative Adams worked on an important law case. Two years earlier, a group of captive Africans had been on the slave ship *Amistad*. The Africans took control of the ship near Cuba. They sailed to the United States, where they were arrested. Adams became their lawyer. He fought for their freedom and won the case. They returned to Africa.

On February 21, 1848, Adams suffered a **stroke** on the floor of the House. Two days later, John Quincy Adams died in the US Capitol. He is buried at United First Parish Church in Quincy.

Adams served his country and earned the nation's respect. He believed all Americans deserved to be free. So, he publicly opposed slavery. Adams is remembered as one of America's greatest **diplomats**. His patriotism helped him make peace with other countries. These contributions helped strengthen the country John Quincy Adams loved.

Throughout his life, Adams kept detailed diaries. These diaries provide much information about the former president.

THE
SLAVES' DREAM.

WRITTEN BY WILLIAM C. CAROLL.

I had a dream, a happy dream, I dreamed that I was free,
And in my own bright land again there was a home for me,
Savannah's tide rushed bravely on, I saw wave roll o'er wave,
And when in full delight I awoke, I found myself a slave,
    And when in full delight I awoke, I found myself a slave.

I never knew a mother's love, though happy were my days,
'Twas by my own dear father's side I sung my simple lays,
He died and heartless strangers came, and o'er him closed the grave,
They tore me weeping from his side, and claimed me as a slave,
    They tore me weeping from his side, and claimed me as a slave.

And this was in a Christain land, where men oft kneel and pray,
The vaunted home of liberty where whip and lash holds sway ;
O, give me back my Georgian cot, it is not wealth I crave,
O, let me live in freedom's light, or die if still a slave.
    O, let me live in freedom's light, or die if still a slave.

THE SLAVES' FUNERAL.

They came to the funeral from plantations round,
    To bury the slave, at the dead hour of night ;
A death-song they sang, as they walked to the ground,
    With pine-torches blazing, to give them their light.
They let him down gently, in the grave dark and deep ;
    On the coffin with earth, from eyes dark and dim,
Fell softly the warm tears, as in love they did weep,
    Death removed the poor slave from all sorrow and sin.

*Andrews', Printer, 38 Chatham St., N. Y., Dealer in Songs, Games,
Toy Books, Motto Verses, &c., Wholesale and Retail.*

A slave song in which the writer
dreams of freedom

BRANCHES OF GOVERNMENT

The US government is divided into three branches. They are the executive, legislative, and judicial branches. This division is called a separation of powers. Each branch has some power over the others. This is called a system of checks and balances.

★ EXECUTIVE BRANCH

The executive branch enforces laws. It is made up of the president, the vice president, and the president's cabinet. The president represents the United States around the world. He or she oversees relations with other countries and signs treaties. The president signs bills into law and appoints officials and federal judges. He or she also leads the military and manages government workers.

★ LEGISLATIVE BRANCH

The legislative branch makes laws, maintains the military, and regulates trade. It also has the power to declare war. This branch consists of the Senate and the House of Representatives. Together, these two houses make up Congress. Each state has two senators. A state's population determines the number of representatives it has.

★ JUDICIAL BRANCH

The judicial branch interprets laws. It consists of district courts, courts of appeals, and the Supreme Court. District courts try cases. If a person disagrees with a trial's outcome, he or she may appeal. If a court of appeals supports the ruling, a person may appeal to the Supreme Court. The Supreme Court also makes sure that laws follow the US Constitution.

THE PRESIDENT ★

★ QUALIFICATIONS FOR OFFICE

To be president, a person must meet three requirements. A candidate must be at least 35 years old and a natural-born US citizen. He or she must also have lived in the United States for at least 14 years.

★ ELECTORAL COLLEGE

The US presidential election is an indirect election. Voters from each state choose electors to represent them in the Electoral College. The number of electors from each state is based on the state's population. Each elector has one electoral vote. Electors are pledged to cast their vote for the candidate who receives the highest number of popular votes in their state. A candidate must receive the majority of Electoral College votes to win.

★ TERM OF OFFICE

Each president may be elected to two four-year terms. Sometimes, a president may only be elected once. This happens if he or she served more than two years of the previous president's term.

The presidential election is held on the Tuesday after the first Monday in November. The president is sworn in on January 20 of the following year. At that time, he or she takes the oath of office:

> *I do solemnly swear (or affirm) that I will faithfully execute the office of President of the United States, and will to the best of my ability, preserve, protect and defend the Constitution of the United States.*

★ LINE OF SUCCESSION ★

The Presidential Succession Act of 1947 defines who becomes president if the president cannot serve. The vice president is first in the line of succession. Next are the Speaker of the House and the President Pro Tempore of the Senate. If none of these individuals is able to serve, the office falls to the president's cabinet members. They would take office in the order in which each department was created:

Secretary of State

Secretary of the Treasury

Secretary of Defense

Attorney General

Secretary of the Interior

Secretary of Agriculture

Secretary of Commerce

Secretary of Labor

Secretary of Health and Human Services

Secretary of Housing and Urban Development

Secretary of Transportation

Secretary of Energy

Secretary of Education

Secretary of Veterans Affairs

Secretary of Homeland Security

While in office, the president receives a salary of $400,000 each year. He or she lives in the White House and has 24-hour Secret Service protection.

The president may travel on a Boeing 747 jet called Air Force One. The airplane can accommodate 76 passengers. It has kitchens, a dining room, sleeping areas, and a conference room. It also has fully equipped offices with the latest communications systems. Air Force One can fly halfway around the world before needing to refuel. It can even refuel in flight!

Air Force One

If the president wishes to travel by car, he or she uses Cadillac One. It has been modified with heavy armor and communications systems. The president takes

Cadillac One along when visiting other countries if secure transportation will be needed.

The president also travels on a helicopter called Marine One. Like the presidential car, Marine One accompanies the president when traveling abroad if necessary.

— Cadillac One —

Sometimes, the president needs to get away and relax with family and friends. Camp David is the official presidential retreat. It is located in the cool, wooded mountains of Maryland. The US Navy maintains the retreat, and the US Marine Corps keeps it secure. The camp offers swimming, tennis, golf, and hiking.

When the president leaves office, he or she receives lifetime Secret Service protection. He or she also receives a yearly pension of $207,800 and funding for office space, supplies, and staff.

— Marine One —

George Washington

Abraham Lincoln

Theodore Roosevelt

	PRESIDENT	PARTY	TOOK OFFICE
1	George Washington	None	April 30, 1789
2	John Adams	Federalist	March 4, 1797
3	Thomas Jefferson	Democratic-Republican	March 4, 1801
4	James Madison	Democratic-Republican	March 4, 1809
5	James Monroe	Democratic-Republican	March 4, 1817
6	John Quincy Adams	Democratic-Republican	March 4, 1825
7	Andrew Jackson	Democrat	March 4, 1829
8	Martin Van Buren	Democrat	March 4, 1837
9	William H. Harrison	Whig	March 4, 1841
10	John Tyler	Whig	April 6, 1841
11	James K. Polk	Democrat	March 4, 1845
12	Zachary Taylor	Whig	March 5, 1849
13	Millard Fillmore	Whig	July 10, 1850
14	Franklin Pierce	Democrat	March 4, 1853
15	James Buchanan	Democrat	March 4, 1857
16	Abraham Lincoln	Republican	March 4, 1861
17	Andrew Johnson	Democrat	April 15, 1865
18	Ulysses S. Grant	Republican	March 4, 1869
19	Rutherford B. Hayes	Republican	March 3, 1877

LEFT OFFICE	TERMS SERVED	VICE PRESIDENT
March 4, 1797	Two	John Adams
March 4, 1801	One	Thomas Jefferson
March 4, 1809	Two	Aaron Burr, George Clinton
March 4, 1817	Two	George Clinton, Elbridge Gerry
March 4, 1825	Two	Daniel D. Tompkins
March 4, 1829	One	John C. Calhoun
March 4, 1837	Two	John C. Calhoun, Martin Van Buren
March 4, 1841	One	Richard M. Johnson
April 4, 1841	Died During First Term	John Tyler
March 4, 1845	Completed Harrison's Term	Office Vacant
March 4, 1849	One	George M. Dallas
July 9, 1850	Died During First Term	Millard Fillmore
March 4, 1853	Completed Taylor's Term	Office Vacant
March 4, 1857	One	William R.D. King
March 4, 1861	One	John C. Breckinridge
April 15, 1865	Served One Term, Died During Second Term	Hannibal Hamlin, Andrew Johnson
March 4, 1869	Completed Lincoln's Second Term	Office Vacant
March 4, 1877	Two	Schuyler Colfax, Henry Wilson
March 4, 1881	One	William A. Wheeler

Franklin D. Roosevelt

John F. Kennedy

Ronald Reagan

	PRESIDENT	PARTY	TOOK OFFICE
20	James A. Garfield	Republican	March 4, 1881
21	Chester Arthur	Republican	September 20, 1881
22	Grover Cleveland	Democrat	March 4, 1885
23	Benjamin Harrison	Republican	March 4, 1889
24	Grover Cleveland	Democrat	March 4, 1893
25	William McKinley	Republican	March 4, 1897
26	Theodore Roosevelt	Republican	September 14, 1901
27	William Taft	Republican	March 4, 1909
28	Woodrow Wilson	Democrat	March 4, 1913
29	Warren G. Harding	Republican	March 4, 1921
30	Calvin Coolidge	Republican	August 3, 1923
31	Herbert Hoover	Republican	March 4, 1929
32	Franklin D. Roosevelt	Democrat	March 4, 1933
33	Harry S. Truman	Democrat	April 12, 1945
34	Dwight D. Eisenhower	Republican	January 20, 1953
35	John F. Kennedy	Democrat	January 20, 1961

LEFT OFFICE	TERMS SERVED	VICE PRESIDENT
September 19, 1881	Died During First Term	Chester Arthur
March 4, 1885	Completed Garfield's Term	Office Vacant
March 4, 1889	One	Thomas A. Hendricks
March 4, 1893	One	Levi P. Morton
March 4, 1897	One	Adlai E. Stevenson
September 14, 1901	Served One Term, Died During Second Term	Garret A. Hobart, Theodore Roosevelt
March 4, 1909	Completed McKinley's Second Term, Served One Term	Office Vacant, Charles Fairbanks
March 4, 1913	One	James S. Sherman
March 4, 1921	Two	Thomas R. Marshall
August 2, 1923	Died During First Term	Calvin Coolidge
March 4, 1929	Completed Harding's Term, Served One Term	Office Vacant, Charles Dawes
March 4, 1933	One	Charles Curtis
April 12, 1945	Served Three Terms, Died During Fourth Term	John Nance Garner, Henry A. Wallace, Harry S. Truman
January 20, 1953	Completed Roosevelt's Fourth Term, Served One Term	Office Vacant, Alben Barkley
January 20, 1961	Two	Richard Nixon
November 22, 1963	Died During First Term	Lyndon B. Johnson

	PRESIDENT	PARTY	TOOK OFFICE
36	Lyndon B. Johnson	Democrat	November 22, 1963
37	Richard Nixon	Republican	January 20, 1969
38	Gerald Ford	Republican	August 9, 1974
39	Jimmy Carter	Democrat	January 20, 1977
40	Ronald Reagan	Republican	January 20, 1981
41	George H.W. Bush	Republican	January 20, 1989
42	Bill Clinton	Democrat	January 20, 1993
43	George W. Bush	Republican	January 20, 2001
44	Barack Obama	Democrat	January 20, 2009
45	Donald Trump	Republican	January 20, 2017

Barack Obama

★ PRESIDENTS MATH GAME ★

Have fun with this presidents math game! First, study the list above and memorize each president's name and number. Then, use math to figure out which president completes each equation below.

1. James Monroe + John Quincy Adams = ?

2. John Quincy Adams + Rutherford B. Hayes = ?

3. Jimmy Carter − John Quincy Adams = ?

Answers: 1. James K. Polk (5 + 6 = 11)
2. William McKinley (6 + 19 = 25)
3. Harry S. Truman (39 − 6 = 33)

LEFT OFFICE	TERMS SERVED	VICE PRESIDENT
January 20, 1969	Completed Kennedy's Term, Served One Term	Office Vacant, Hubert H. Humphrey
August 9, 1974	Completed First Term, Resigned During Second Term	Spiro T. Agnew, Gerald Ford
January 20, 1977	Completed Nixon's Second Term	Nelson A. Rockefeller
January 20, 1981	One	Walter Mondale
January 20, 1989	Two	George H.W. Bush
January 20, 1993	One	Dan Quayle
January 20, 2001	Two	Al Gore
January 20, 2009	Two	Dick Cheney
January 20, 2017	Two	Joe Biden
		Mike Pence

★ WRITE TO THE PRESIDENT ★

You may write to the president at:

The White House
1600 Pennsylvania Avenue NW
Washington, DC 20500

You may email the president at:

www.whitehouse.gov/contact

★ GLOSSARY ★

American Revolution—from 1775 to 1783. A war for independence between Great Britain and its North American colonies. The colonists won and created the United States of America.

cabinet—a group of advisers chosen by the president to lead government departments.

Constitution—the laws that govern the United States.

Democrat—a member of the Democratic political party. When John Quincy Adams was president, Democrats supported farmers and landowners.

Democratic-Republican—a member of the Democratic-Republican political party. During the early 1800s, Democratic-Republicans believed in weak national government and strong state government.

diplomat—an official who represents his or her country's government in a foreign country. Something relating to a diplomat is diplomatic.

embargo—an order of a government banning the departure of commercial ships from its ports.

fluent—able to speak clearly and easily in a particular language.

inauguration (ih-naw-gyuh-RAY-shuhn)—a ceremony in which a person is sworn into office. Something relating to an inauguration is inaugural.

massacre—the murdering of many people.

National Republican—a member of the National Republican political party. National Republicans opposed Andrew Jackson and believed in Henry Clay's program of high tariffs, internal improvements, and a national bank.

observatory—an institution whose primary purpose is making observations of happenings of nature.

riot—a sometimes violent disturbance caused by a large group of people.

running mate—a candidate running for a lower-rank position on an election ticket, especially the candidate for vice president.

secretary of state—a member of the president's cabinet who handles relations with other countries.

secretary of the treasury—a member of the president's cabinet that heads the US Department of the Treasury. The secretary advises the president on financial policies and reports to Congress on the nation's finances. The secretary of the treasury is the US government's chief financial officer.

secretary of war—a member of the president's cabinet who handles the nation's defense. This position was replaced by the secretary of the army in 1947.

Speaker of the House—the highest-ranking member of the party with the majority in Congress.

stroke—a sudden loss of consciousness, sensation, and voluntary motion. This attack of paralysis is caused by a rupture to a blood vessel of the brain, often caused by a blood clot.

tariff—the taxes a government puts on imported or exported goods.

War of 1812—from 1812 to 1815. A war fought between the United States and Great Britain over shipping rights and the capture of US soldiers.

ONLINE RESOURCES

Booklinks
NONFICTION NETWORK
FREE! ONLINE NONFICTION RESOURCES

To learn more about John Quincy Adams, please visit **abdobooklinks.com** or scan this QR code. These links are routinely monitored and updated to provide the most current information available.

★ INDEX ★